101 ANIMAL RECORDS

ISBN 978-0-545-42796-8

12 11 10 9 8 7 6 5 4 3 2 1   13 14 15 16 17 18/0

Printed in the U.S.A.   40
First printing, January 2013
Book design by Kay Petronio

101 ANIMAL RECORDS

BY Melvin + Gilda Berger

SCHOLASTIC

For many years, the Abingdon tortoise was the rarest of all living creatures. In fact, there was only one in the entire world! People called him Lonesome George. This Abingdon tortoise was the last of many giant land turtles that once lived on Pinta, a small island off the coast of South America. The species became endangered after goats, which settlers had brought to the island, destroyed most of the tortoises' food. In June 2012, Lonesome George died at the age of 100, making the species extinct.

#1 ABINGDON TORTOISE:
Last of Its Kind

#2 AFRICAN ELEPHANT: Largest Animal

The most massive land animal in the world is the male African elephant. Its record height is 13 feet (4 m), with a weight of over 11 tons (10,000 kg). That is about twice as tall and six times as heavy as an average-sized automobile! Male African elephants also hold records for the longest tusks and the largest ears of all animals, as well as the biggest brains of any land animal. Male Asian elephants and both kinds of female elephants are smaller than the record-setting male African elephant.

The African wild dog catches about 70% of all animals it hunts. It mostly preys on large animals, such as antelopes, gazelles, and wildebeests. When an African wild dog spots its prey, it takes up the chase with several others in its pack. They race along at speeds over 35 miles per hour (56 kph). If the lead dog gets tired, it falls back and other dogs surge ahead. Chased prey rarely escapes this most successful mammal predator.

#3 AFRICAN WILD DOG:
Most Successful Hunter

#4 ANOPHELES MOSQUITO: Greatest Killer Insect

The female *Anopheles* mosquito spreads malaria, a very serious disease that kills anywhere from 600,000 to more than 1 million people a year! After the female *Anopheles* mosquito bites someone with malaria, she sucks up a drop of blood that contains some of the tiny parasites that cause the disease. Then, when she bites a healthy person, some of those parasites enter the victim's bloodstream. This causes the often fatal disease.

The archerfish uses its mouth like a water pistol to catch its dinner. Its prey includes insects and spiders that rest on branches over the shallow, tropical waters where the archerfish lives. When the fish spots a bug, it shoots a thin, powerful stream of water in its direction. The spray strikes the bug and knocks it down into the water. The fish quickly swallows it up. An archerfish can shoot the water as far as 5 feet (1.5 m)—and almost always hits its target!

#5 ARCHERFISH:
Sharpest Shooter

#6 ARCTIC TERN: Champion Migrator

The Arctic tern is a seabird that travels farther than any other animal. It spends the summer months in the Arctic, the most northern part of Earth. When autumn comes, the tern flies to Antarctica, the southernmost part. In spring, the tern starts its journey back to the Arctic. The round trip can be as long as 31,000 miles (50,000 km)! In its lifetime, an Arctic tern can cover as many as 750,000 miles (1.2 million km)!

An axolotl salamander is often called an amphibian that never grew up. Amphibians are animals with backbones that live part of their life on land and part in water. Most grow from egg to larva to adult, but the axolotl stays a larva all its life! Among its very strange features are the feathery gills sticking up from its head and a "happy face" that never changes. The axolotl can swim, though it mostly walks on lake bottoms.

#7 AXOLOTL:
Strangest Amphibian

BADGER:
#8 Speediest Digger

A badger can dig faster than any other mammal—including a person with a shovel! Built for digging, badgers have strong shoulders, sharp-clawed feet, and partly webbed front toes to scoop up the soil. These master diggers first make underground tunnels to find prey. Later, they expand the tunnels, which they use as a place to sleep and raise their young. Someone has even said they once saw a badger dig through the paving of a Midwest parking lot and disappear underground in two minutes!

11

Bald eagles are large birds of prey that usually build colossal nests near the tops of trees. Both males and females, working together, make the nests mainly of sticks. They line the bottoms with a soft layer of feathers. The largest nest on record was found in Florida. It measured 9 1/2 feet (2.9 m) across, 20 feet (6.1 m) deep, and weighed nearly 3 tons (2,700 kg)! Because they mostly eat fish, bald eagles often place their nests in trees near water. It takes a pair of eagles up to three months to finish a nest.

#9 BALD EAGLE:
Largest Bird Nest

BASILISK LIZARD: Largest Walker on Water

#10

The basilisk lizard has the most amazing ability to sprint across water! It lives in trees alongside rivers and streams in the rain forests of Central America. When threatened, it drops down from a tree and darts away on the water's surface. Its big hind feet have flaps of skin between the toes. The flaps trap bubbles of air underneath, keeping the lizard afloat. After a while, the lizard slows down and starts to sink. To continue its escape, the lizard switches to swimming.

From the tip of its bill to the end of its tail, the bee hummingbird is just over 2 inches (5 cm) long—about the size of an eraser! Everything about this bird is tiny. It weighs less than a penny. The nest it builds is no bigger than half a walnut shell. The eggs that the female lays are as small as coffee beans. Bee hummingbirds may be tiny, but they are also tough. Despite their small size, they fight off large predators, such as hawks.

#11 BEE HUMMINGBIRD:
Smallest Bird

BLACK MAMBA: #12 Fastest Land Snake

The African black mamba is the swiftest of all land snakes. In short bursts, it is able to reach speeds of up to 12 miles per hour (19 kph). The black mamba races along the ground with its head high and the front of its body lifted. It mostly uses its great speed to escape danger, not to hunt prey. But mambas can be very dangerous. One account from 2006 tells of a mamba bringing down an adult female elephant!

The blue-ringed octopus is small, but extremely dangerous. In fact, this octopus is one of the most poisonous creatures in the sea. Each one is believed to have enough poison, or venom, to paralyze ten adult men. The octopus attacks only when threatened by someone picking it up or stepping on it. Then, it turns bright yellow with blue ring markings—and it strikes. Just one painless bite with its parrotlike beak can paralyze or kill a person in minutes.

#13 BLUE-RINGED OCTOPUS:
Deadliest Sea Creature

#14 BLUE WHALE: Largest Animal That Ever Lived

Blue whales are mammals that break every record for length and weight. Reaching an average length of 100 feet (30 m), the blue whale is longer than three buses. It weighs 200 tons (180,000 kg)—more than 20 African elephants! Everything about this mighty beast is stupendous: Its heart is the size of a small automobile! Fifty people could stand on its tongue! You could crawl through its main artery! To top it all, its body is as tall as a two-story building!

Of all the animals in the ocean, the bottlenose dolphin is the most intelligent. Its huge brain is even bigger than that of a human! Dolphins keep in touch with one another by means of a special "language" made up of squeaks, clicks, and whistles. They have been known to rescue people lost at sea. A familiar animal in aquariums, dolphins can perform many tricks, from catching balls to singing or painting.

#15 BOTTLENOSE DOLPHIN:
Smartest Sea Animal

#16 BOWERBIRD:
Most Romantic Bird

The male bowerbird has a whole bag of delightful ways to win a mate. First, he decorates a small section of the forest floor with brightly colored bits of plastic, string, feathers, pebbles, berries, or shells. When a female arrives, the male dances and sings. He fluffs up his feathers, buzzes loudly, and struts wildly back and forth. The males who decorate, dance, and sing most skillfully usually get the female bowerbirds of their dreams!

This tiny mammal, the bumblebee bat, is about as big as a bee and only a little heavier. At just over 1 inch (2.5 cm) in length, it is about as long as the top part of an adult's thumb. A fraction of an ounce (2 g) in weight, the bumblebee bat is lighter than a Ping-Pong ball! The bat spends most of its time roosting in the deepest and darkest caves of southern Asia. For short periods at dawn and dusk, it emerges to hunt for food, such as insects and spiders.

#17 BUMBLEBEE BAT:
Smallest Mammal

#18 CAECILIAN: Best Amphibian Mom

Caecilians are long, burrowing amphibians that live in the tropics. After the eggs hatch, the mother takes three days to grow a new layer of skin rich in fat and nutrients. When the skin is ripe, the young have a feeding frenzy. The mother waits calmly as they peel and eat her skin! In three days, she grows another skin. Once again, the young devour it. The good mother skin-feeds them this way for about three months!

The carpet viper kills more people than any other snake in the world! Found mostly in Africa and India, the carpet viper is small and not easily seen—until it is too late. In addition to moving fast, the snake is short-tempered and often strikes without warning. The carpet viper bites hard and often, delivering a great deal of venom with each bite. Just one bite from a carpet viper can cause uncontrollable bleeding and even death.

#19 CARPET VIPER:
Most Dangerous Snake

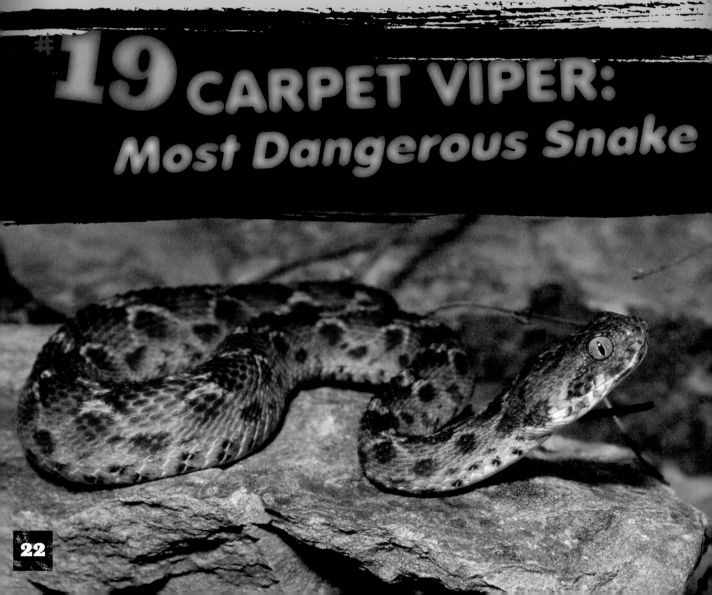

#20 CASSOWARY: Deadliest Claws

Cassowaries are massive flightless birds of Australia and New Guinea. They are shy birds, able to disappear before anyone even knows they are there. But any creature that gets too close can suffer painful wounds. Cassowaries have powerful legs and three toes with sharp, pointed nails on each foot. A kick from a cassowary can cripple. A slash with a claw can rip through flesh and bone.

23

Although they are best known for their unusual ability to change skin color, chameleons also take the prize for their amazing eyes. Each eye moves and focuses by itself. One eye can look forward while the other looks backward. Thus, the chameleon can use one eye to look for prey while the other eye looks out for predators. It also can see in all directions—front, back, up, and down. Think of this the next time you try to sneak up on a chameleon!

#21 CHAMELEON:
Most Amazing Eyes

#22 CHEETAH: Fastest Sprinter

The cheetah outruns all other animals—but only for short distances, or sprints. Its speed has been compared to that of a high-powered sports car. The cheetah can accelerate from a standing position to 65 miles an hour (105 kph) in just 3 seconds! Many reach their top speed when chasing antelopes, gazelles, or wildebeests across the African grasslands. But they only keep this speed for less than one minute—the length of an average chase.

Chimpanzees show their high intelligence in many ways. In the wild, chimpanzees use tools to solve problems. They use stones to crack nuts; long, thin twigs to pull termites from their mounds; short, small twigs to clean their teeth; and leaves squeezed into balls to soak up drinking water. In the lab, chimpanzees have learned to solve math problems, use computers, and even communicate with humans using sign language!

#23 CHIMPANZEE: Smartest Land Animal

#24 CHINESE GIANT SALAMANDER: Largest Amphibian

Most Chinese giant salamanders are about the size and weight of an average eight-year-old. But a salamander recently found in China is a record breaker. It measures 6 feet (1.8 m) in length and weighs 143 pounds (64 kg). That's almost as big as a full-grown adult man! These huge creatures spend their entire lives in water, preying at night on frogs and fish. Called living fossils, Chinese giant salamanders have been on Earth for 350 million years!

Male cicadas make extremely shrill sounds to attract females. When many call together, they produce the loudest of all insect sounds. They may be heard up to a quarter mile (402 m) away! Some compare the sounds to a buzz saw. The cicada makes the noise by tightening and loosening muscles in its abdomen several hundred times a second. Each kind of cicada has its own "song." Large groups often sing together from trees or bushes.

#25 CICADA:
Loudest Insect

#26 CLEANER FISH: Most Helpful Fish

Cleaner fish come to the aid of many creatures that live in the sea. These small fish live on coral reefs, where they set up special "cleaning stations." Other kinds of fish swim over to these cleaning stations and open their mouths wide. The cleaner fish feeds on any food scraps or parasites it finds there. Sometimes fish wait in a line to have their mouths cleaned. One cleaner fish can help as many as 2,500 fish a day—almost two a minute!

The common tenrec is a small mammal found on islands in the Indian Ocean. Females can give birth to litters of as many as 32 young—more than any other mammal. More usual are litters of between 10 and 20. The mothers can nurse up to 29 young at one time, which is another record. The common tenrec looks like a hedgehog with stiff, needlelike spines along its back. If threatened, it may scream, straighten its spines, jump up, and bite.

#27 COMMON TENREC: *Largest Litter*

#28 DESERT LOCUST: Most Destructive Insect

Desert locusts cause terrible damage on farms growing crops in Africa, the Middle East, and Asia. Each locust can eat its own weight in food every day! Immense swarms of locusts move across the land devouring all plants in their path. By wiping out entire crops, they cause dreadful human misery and starvation. A single large swarm contains about 80 billion locusts! The largest swarm ever recorded numbered an estimated 250 billion insects.

Desert tortoises are clumsy, slow-moving turtles that are found only in the deserts of the southwestern United States. (Tortoises are turtles that live only on dry land.) The desert tortoises have round, stumpy feet, like elephants, which makes it very hard for them to move fast. Their large, heavy shells also slow them down. Most cannot cover more than about 10 feet (3 m) in a minute. At this rate, it can take them up to 9 hours to walk just 1 mile (1.6 km)!

#29 DESERT TORTOISE:
Slowest Turtle

#30 DRAGONFLY: Fastest-Flying Insect

Scientists consider the dragonfly the fastest insect, even though its exact speed is very hard to measure. According to many experts, the most reliable level flight-speed record for the dragonfly is 36 miles an hour (58 kph). Even more amazing is the record for downhill flight—an astounding 59 miles an hour (94 kph)! All dragonflies need to fly very fast in order to catch insects, their main source of food, in midair.

The electric eel is a snakelike fish that can give an electric shock strong enough to stun or kill prey in the water. Along its long tail are some 6,000 special cells that store electricity like tiny batteries. When the eel finds a fish to feed on, it fires up the cells. Out shoots a charge as high as 650 volts—more than five times the voltage of a wall socket. Electric eels, which swim in the rivers of South America, can be as long as 8 feet (2.4 m) and can weigh up to 44 pounds (20 kg).

#31 ELECTRIC EEL:
Most Shocking Animal

#32 EMPEROR PENGUIN: Best Bird Dad

The male emperor penguin sits near the female as she lays an egg on the ice. She immediately rolls the egg onto the male's feet to keep it from freezing. He covers the egg with a flap of skin and the female goes away to get food. For two months the father keeps the egg warm. He doesn't eat and loses about half his weight. After the egg hatches, the father feeds the chick "milk" from his throat. On the mother's return, she feeds the chick and the dad leaves to find food.

While the mustache is the emperor tamarin monkey's most striking feature, no one has been able to explain its purpose. What is known, however, is how the monkey got its name. Many years ago, someone joked that the monkey looked like Wilhelm II, emperor of Germany, who indeed had an equally grand mustache. Since the joke was repeated many times, emperor became part of this monkey's name.

#33 EMPEROR TAMARIN MONKEY: *Grandest Mustache*

#34 FAIRYFLY: Smallest Insect

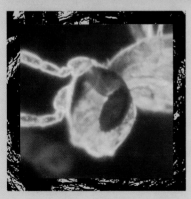

The tiny insect that people call a fairyfly is not a fly at all. It's a wasp! The smallest fairyfly on record is only a tiny, tiny fraction of an inch (mm) long. In fact, a fairyfly is so small that you actually need a microscope to see the parts of its body! Females are usually bigger than males and are poor fliers. Some kinds of male fairyflies have no wings and do not fly at all. Males and females are usually carried along on currents of air.

The flying dragon is a lizard with folds of skin that spread out to make "wings." Although this lizard has no power of flight, it uses these so-called wings to glide through the air as far as 65 feet (20 m)! A single flight could carry it from the pitcher's mound to past home plate on a baseball diamond. When folded against its body, the wings' dull color makes them hard to see. But when opened, they sparkle with bright colors.

#35 FLYING DRAGON:
Best "Flying" Lizard

#36 FLYING FISH:
Best Glider

Flying fish are fast swimmers and even more amazing fliers. When being chased by predators in the water, they start swimming as fast as 20 miles an hour (32 kph). Then, with a flick of their strong tails, they take off into the air. With their four winglike fins spread wide, they glide away. The longest flight is about a quarter mile (400 m)! Because swordfish, tunas, and other large enemies cannot fly, the flying fish easily escape them.

The frogfish gulps down food more quickly than any other animal. Its eating speed has been compared to the sucking action of a vacuum cleaner. The frogfish hides near a coral reef and waits for a victim. The lure on its head tricks other fish into coming closer. As one approaches, the frogfish snaps its mouth open to 12 times its normal size. This creates a superpowerful vacuum. Whoosh! The prey disappears into its mouth in only one six-thousandth of a second!

#37 FROGFISH: Fastest Eater

#38 GABOON VIPER: Longest Fangs

The longest, sharpest teeth, or fangs, of any snake belong to Africa's Gaboon viper. Each fang measures about 2 inches (5 cm), which is about the length of your pointer finger! Inside the hollow fangs are canals through which powerful poison, or venom, flows. Most of the time, the fangs are folded back against the top of the snake's mouth. But when the viper attacks, the fangs snap down and inject more venom per bite than any other snake's.

Galápagos tortoises are the longest-lived reptiles in the world, as well as the largest turtles. When Charles Darwin visited the Galápagos Islands in 1835, he collected three of these tortoises. Experts determined that one of them, named Harriet, was born around 1830. Harriet died in 2006 after 175 birthdays! Other Galápagos tortoises are believed to have lived just as long.

#39 GALÁPAGOS TORTOISE: Most Birthdays

#40 GIANT ANTEATER: Strangest Tongue

The giant anteater has a long, thin, sticky tongue—a remarkable 24 inches (61 cm) in length! It is the perfect tool for catching ants, which are the anteater's main food. The giant anteater sticks its lengthy tongue in and out of anthills about 150 times a minute. In this way, it is able to catch about 30,000 ants in a single day! Found in Central and South America, the anteater swallows the ants stuck on its tongue without chewing, since it has no teeth.

The largest giant clam ever found reached a length of 4 feet (1.2 m). That's big enough to hold a human being! Giant clams are sometimes called killer clams because of the legend that some swimmers have been caught inside them. But this is not true. Giant clams close their shells very slowly, giving anyone inside plenty of time to escape. These clams live on coral reefs in warm, shallow waters of the South Pacific and Indian oceans.

#41 GIANT CLAM: Largest Shellfish

#42 GIANT HAWK MOTH:
Longest Insect Tongue

The giant hawk moth uses its extremely long tongue, or feeding tube, to gather nectar from flowers. In 1862, Charles Darwin discovered that the nectar in star orchids was at the bottom of their thin, foot-long (30 cm) flowers. Darwin guessed that there must be a moth with a tongue long enough to reach that nectar. Many years later, the giant hawk moth was found. Sure enough, its tongue is 11 inches (28 cm) long and it feeds on nectar from the star orchid!

The giant Pacific octopus is one of the most extraordinary sea creatures in the world. Each of its eight arms, which are attached to its head, is more than 6 feet (2 m) in length. Its entire body can stretch out to reach 25 feet (8 m) across and it can weigh as much as 400 pounds (180 kg)! Yet at birth this huge creature is no bigger than a single grain of rice!

#43 GIANT PACIFIC OCTOPUS:
Largest Octopus

#44 GIANT PANDA: Fussiest Eater

The giant panda lives almost entirely on bamboo stems and leaves. Each panda eats about 28 pounds (13 kg) of bamboo a day. And most pandas spend half a day eating! Large molar teeth and strong jaw muscles crush the tough plants easily and well. The giant panda is an excellent tree climber and swimmer. In the wild, it is found in very small numbers only in the cool, damp, high-mountain bamboo forests of central China.

The giant squid needs huge eyes to survive in the very lowest depths of the ocean, where it lives. At this level, the water is almost completely dark. To help it see in these conditions, the giant squid has the largest eyes of any animal in the world—about 11 inches (28 cm) across. That makes the eyes bigger than dinner plates, with eyeballs larger than basketballs! At a record length of 59 feet (18 m), the giant squid is also the largest animal without a backbone.

#45 GIANT SQUID:
Biggest Eyes

#46 GILA MONSTER: Most Feared Lizard

The Gila monster is known as the most poisonous lizard in the world. But its venom is actually quite mild and the lizard uses it mainly to protect itself, not to attack. Some think the animal has poisonous breath or that it can spit venom. Neither is true. While some humans have died from Gila monster bites, most survive with such symptoms as pain, weakness, and vomiting. The Gila monster makes its home in the southwestern United States and Mexico.

The most extreme fact about the giraffe is obvious: It is the tallest of all animals. But it also runs faster than a horse, can go longer without water than a camel, and can kill a lion with one kick! The record height for giraffes is 19 feet (6 m), which includes its horns! If placed next to a house, it would reach above the second floor. A giraffe's neck is almost 20 times the length of your neck, yet both have exactly seven bones!

#47 GIRAFFE:
Tallest Animal

#48 GIRAFFE WEEVIL: Longest Insect Neck

Tiny giraffe weevils have bizarrely long necks. The male mainly uses its neck, which is about three times as long as a female's, for fighting other males. For a long time scientists believed that the male also used its neck in nest building. But in 2011, experts saw a female use her neck to build a nest. She laid a single egg on a leaf and rolled it up into a tube for protection. After the egg hatched, the larva ate the leaf—its first food.

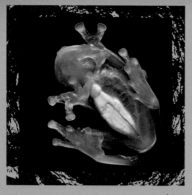

This see-through frog takes its name from the skin over its belly. It is transparent, just like clear plastic! When the frog is belly up, you can see its insides—bones, organs, and even blood vessels. Except for the belly, the glass frog is covered with green skin. Glass frogs also have a strange way of raising their young. The females lay their eggs in tree leaves over streams or creeks. When the eggs hatch, the tadpoles drop down into the water—and swim away!

#49 GLASS FROG: Most Transparent Amphibian

GOLDEN POISON
#50 DART FROG:
Deadliest Frog

The small, pretty, and very colorful golden poison dart frog carries a most toxic poison in its skin. The poison from just one of these frogs is enough to kill 10 people! Just touching a frog with bare hands can cause death. Scientists who handle these frogs wear thick gloves. Natives in the tropical rain forests of Central and South America use the poison to coat the tips of their arrows. One hit by a poisoned arrow can bring down a large animal in seconds!

The goliath beetle claims the title of heavyweight champion of the insect world. The record weight for an adult male is about 4 ounces (113 g)—much like a Whopper hamburger! The goliath beetle's length is as impressive as its weight. The insect can measure a full 5 inches (13 cm) from the tip of its horn to the end of its body. Like Goliath, the giant warrior in the Bible, this huge beetle is a fighter. Often it grabs opponents by the horns and lifts them into the air.

#51 GOLIATH BEETLE:
Heaviest Insect

#52 GOLIATH FROG: Largest Frog

Most frogs can fit in the palm of your hand—but not the goliath frog. This huge amphibian is almost as big as a house cat! It can grow to be a foot long (30 cm) and top the scale at about 7 pounds (3 kg). A giant goliath frog starts life as a small, very ordinary tadpole. But as time goes on, it just keeps growing bigger and bigger. One amazing record-breaking goliath frog was found in 1989. At 14 1/2 inches (37 cm) long, it weighed over 8 pounds (4 kg)!

The hagfish looks like a snake and has no scales. Yet this long, thin creature is a fish that lives in very deep water. Its body is covered with glands that produce great amounts of thick, sticky slime. When in danger, the hagfish releases enough slime to cover its entire body. The slippery coating protects the hagfish from predators by forming a cocoon that clogs the enemies' gills if they come too close. If its own nostrils fill with the slime, the hagfish sneezes it out!

#53 HAGFISH: Slimiest Fish

#54 HIPPOPOTAMUS: Biggest Mouth

A hippopotamus can open its mouth up to 4 feet (1.2 m) wide. That's big enough for a seven-year-old human to stand inside! Most often, the hippo opens its mouth extremely wide to yawn, eat, or frighten another hippopotamus away. If the other hippo does not flee, the two may go nose to nose, slashing each other with their two long, tusklike canine teeth. The hippos sometimes continue fighting until one is killed.

Hoatzins of South America are attractive tropical birds that look like plump pheasants. But don't let their good looks fool you. If you get close to one, you'll find that they smell awful. They are, by far, the smelliest of all birds! For that reason, hoatzins have been nicknamed "stink birds." Their body odor smells like cow manure. It comes from the hoatzins' diet of green leaves that ferment as they are digested. People rarely hunt them for food because they taste as bad as they smell.

#55 HOATZIN:
Smelliest Bird

#56 HONEYBEE:
Most Useful Insect

Honeybees make honey, which humans eat, and wax, which they use to make things. But, even more important, bees carry pollen from one plant to another, which helps many fruits and vegetables grow. This is called pollination. Of the 6 million different insects in the world, bees are the only ones that help produce food that humans and many kinds of animals can eat. In the United States alone, bees help grow more than 100 crops, from apples to zucchinis.

Horned lizards have the strangest way of defending themselves. When threatened, they squirt foul-tasting blood from the corners of their eyes for a distance of more than a yard (1 m)! The stream of blood both scares and confuses their enemies. All but the very bravest predators give up and run away. But shooting blood is a last resort. First these lizards will change skin color, puff up their bodies to look larger, and jump toward the enemy with a loud *H-i-sssss!*

#57 HORNED LIZARD:
Weirdest Defense

#58 HOWLER MONKEY: Loudest Land Animal

The piercing cries of howler monkeys can be heard as far away as 3 miles (5 km) in the tropical rain forests of Latin America where they live. At dawn and at dusk, these monkeys use their supersized voices to keep their group together and to protect their territories. Howler monkeys spend their whole lives in the treetops and are hard to spot from the ground. But their loud cries make them easy prey for hunters, who often hear them before they see them.

For many years, the ivory-billed woodpecker made its home in the swampy forests of the southeastern United States. Gradually, however, this bird became very rare. By the 1920s, experts believed it had disappeared altogether. In the 1930s and 1940s, there were a few new sightings. Then, between 2002 and 2009, several more birds were spotted. But these reports were never confirmed. Today, most experts consider the ivory-billed woodpecker to be probably—or definitely—extinct.

#59 IVORY-BILLED WOODPECKER:
Most Mysterious Animal

#60 KANGAROO: Farthest Leaper

The kangaroo is a timid animal that depends on speed to escape its enemies. Hopping quickly on its two strong hind legs, the fastest known kangaroo made a record-breaking leap of 42 feet (13 m)! That is much farther than the best human running long-jump record of less than 30 feet (9 m). While kangaroos are known for their long leaps, they also jump amazingly high. The record height of 10 feet (3 m) was set by a kangaroo fleeing a pack of hunting dogs.

The koala spends up to 18 out of every 24 hours asleep in the branches of a eucalyptus tree! Although extremely sleepy and very slow-moving, the koala is quick to attack any person or animal that comes too close. It's awake mainly at night, when it feeds only on leaves of the eucalyptus tree. Still, it eats over 2 pounds (1 kg) of leaves a day. A koala rarely drinks water, since it gets all the water it needs from the eucalyptus leaves.

#61 KOALA:
Sleepiest Mammal

#62 KOMODO DRAGON: Most Colossal Lizard

Komodo dragons are not huge monsters of fiction. But they are the largest of all lizards on Earth. The longest measure 10 feet (3 m), which is longer than a Ping-Pong table! And the heaviest weigh 300 pounds (136 kg), which is about double the weight of an adult man.

Nor do Komodo dragons breathe fire like make-believe dragons. Instead, they have deadly saliva. Each bite contains some 50 different kinds of poisonous germs.

Everyone knows that turtles are very slow. But that is not true of the leatherback, the world's largest sea turtle. When chased by an enemy, such as a large shark or a killer whale, the leatherback uses its huge front flippers to swim away superfast. Its highest speed is an astounding 22 miles an hour (35 kph)! Like other reptiles, the leatherback breathes air. But it can dive deeper than any other sea turtle—to a record depth of about 3/4 mile (1.2 km).

#63 LEATHERBACK TURTLE:
Swiftest Turtle

#64 LION: Most Social Big Cat

Among the big cats, only lions live in groups, called prides. Most of the other big cats—tigers, leopards, cheetahs, cougars, and jaguars—live alone. A pride of lions can be made up of about a dozen females (mothers, sisters, and cousins), their young, and a small number of unrelated males. The females of each pride hunt together, share their prey, and help raise one another's cubs. Males guard the pride and defend their territory against other lions.

Many mayflies go through their whole adult life cycle in just one day! This is as long as it takes for them to mate, lay eggs in a stream or lake, and die. The eggs hatch into young mayflies, which go through several stages while clinging to underwater plants or rocks. After about two years, the growing mayflies swim to the water's surface. Here they develop wings and fly away. The adults then pass through their daylong life cycle.

#65 MAYFLY: Shortest Insect Life Span

MIDGE:
#66 Fastest Insect Wingbeat

The midge is often called a no-see-um because it is tiny and beats its wings so fast that it is almost invisible. Scientists estimate that this tiny insect flaps its wings up and down more than 1,000 times a second! Their high-speed flight lets midges land on humans or other mammals, take a quick sip of blood, and escape before being seen, felt, or swatted. Often, large numbers of midges form a swarm. Their rapid wingbeats produce a soft humming sound.

Millipedes look like worms with many legs. Their name means "a thousand legs," though most millipedes have fewer than 300. Recently, a millipede with 750 legs turned up in California and set a record! You might think that an animal with hundreds of legs would be quick on its feet. But this is not so. Millipedes actually move very slowly over the ground as they search for the dead plants and leaves that make up most of their diet.

#67 MILLIPEDE:
Most Legs

#68 MUDSKIPPERS: Most Land-Loving Fish

Mudskippers are fish that spend much of their time on land, not in water! Their fins are like legs, which make them able to move about quickly on land. During high tide, they leave the water and climb onto rocks or roots. Then, as the tide goes out, the mudskippers walk or skip across the mud looking for bits of food to eat. Out of water, they breathe through their skin and get oxygen from the water they have stored in special body cavities.

The 3-foot-long (1-m-long), thick dark brown hairs of the musk ox reach almost to the ground. Someone once said the animals look like "huge dust mops on hooves." Eskimos in Alaska call them *oomingmaks*, which means "animals with skin like a beard." Thanks to its stiff, coarse outer coat and woolly undercoat, the musk ox is able to survive farther north than any other hoofed animal on the planet. The wool of its undercoat is almost ten times warmer than sheep's wool!

#69 MUSK OX:
Shaggiest Hair

#70 OCEAN SUNFISH: Most Eggs

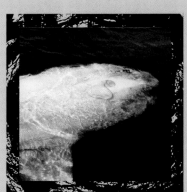

The ocean sunfish lays an astonishing 300 million eggs at a time. That is more eggs than any other animal! The ocean sunfish, which is found in tropical and temperate waters, is also the heaviest of all bony fish. Strange to look at, it has a huge head with fins on top and bottom, as well as a rounded tail. The fish got its name from the way it lies flat on the ocean's surface as though sunbathing.

Among animals with backbones, the bigger you are, usually the longer you live. The olm, which lives in caves in southern Europe, is a notable exception. This tiny, pink-skinned, blind salamander weighs only a fraction of an ounce (20 grams). Yet it can live to be over 100 years old! No one is sure why. It may be that there are no predators in the caves in which it lives. Or its body may just age very slowly. Scientists are working to solve this mystery.

OLM:
#71 Longest-Living Amphibian

#72 ORANGUTAN: Heaviest Tree Dweller

Orangutans are bigger than all other tree-dwelling animals. Males weigh up to 220 pounds (100 kg)—more than extra-large-sized men. Yet, despite their weight, orangutans spend most of their lives in the trees of tropical rain forests. Using their extremely long, powerful arms, they swing and climb from tree to tree in search of food—mainly fruit, leaves, and insects. When the sun starts to set, orangutans build nests in the trees out of branches and go to sleep.

Everything about the ostrich is extremely large. It can grow to be 9 feet (2.7 m) tall with a top weight of 345 pounds (156 kg). That's taller and heavier than a huge professional football player. The ostrich's running record of 45 miles an hour (72 kph) is about twice as fast as the Olympic speed record. Each ostrich leg is about 4 feet (1.2 m) long, which is equal to the height of a first grader. Even the ostrich egg is stupendous. Each one weighs as much as two dozen chicken eggs!

#73 OSTRICH: Biggest Bird

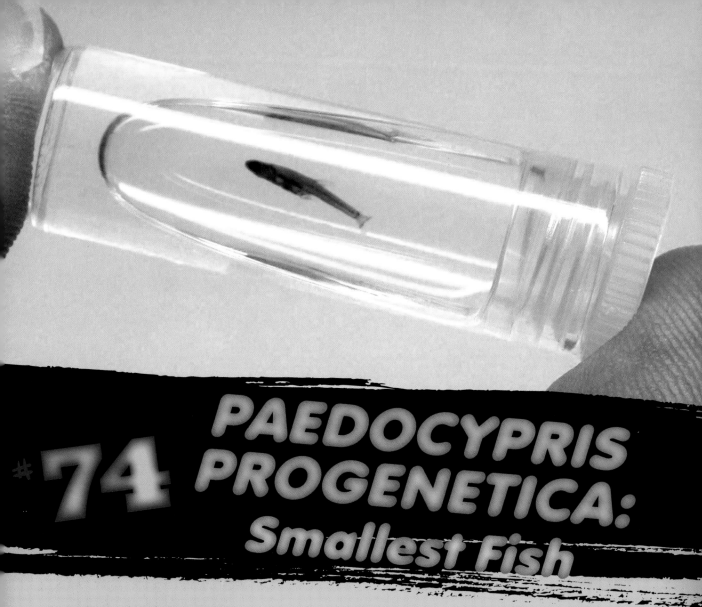

#74 PAEDOCYPRIS PROGENETICA: Smallest Fish

The tiniest fish on record has one of the longest names, *Paedocypris progenetica*. With a see-through body and a visible skeleton, this fish takes the prize as smallest among all animals with backbones. A fully grown *Paedocypris* is just one-third of an inch (7.9 mm) from nose to tail, or about the size of a mosquito! Found in the swamps of southeastern Asia, the fish feeds on animals even smaller than itself floating in the water.

When diving to catch other birds in midair, peregrine falcons can reach up to 200 miles an hour (320 kph). This is thought to be the top speed any animal can reach! These fastest animals in the world often live on high cliffs over seacoasts. From here, a peregrine spots its prey, plummets down, and strikes the victim with a forceful blow. Having stunned or killed it, the falcon then swoops around and snatches the bird in its claws.

#75 PEREGRINE FALCON: Fastest Animal

#76 PIRANHA: Meanest Freshwater Fish

The razor-toothed piranha, found in the rivers of South America, is believed to be the most ferocious of all fish. It viciously attacks any creature, no matter its size. Within minutes, it uses its powerful jaws and supersharp teeth to tear a victim's flesh to shreds. Even fishermen who catch piranhas have to be careful that they don't lose a finger—or more. Piranha teeth are so sharp that South American natives sometimes shave with them!

Among carnivores, or meat eaters, polar bears are the largest and heaviest land animals in the world. The record holder reached a height of 11 feet 2 inches (3.4 m) and a weight around 1,700 pounds (771 kg)! Polar bears mainly hunt seals, and can eat 100 pounds (45 kg) in just one meal! When hungry, though, they will feed on any meat they can find, from dead whales to seabirds. To spot prey, these huge Arctic bears sometimes stand up on their hind legs.

#77 POLAR BEAR:
Greatest Land Carnivore

#78 PRONGHORN: Best Distance Runner

Over time, pronghorns have evolved into the fastest-running animals for long distances. Prolonged running is the pronghorns' only way to escape predators such as wolves and coyotes. One champion pronghorn was clocked at the amazing speed of 61 miles an hour (98 kph) for a short distance. But most can keep a steady speed of about 45 miles an hour (72 kph) as they race across the open grasslands of western North America.

The average length of a reticulated python is about 17 feet (5 m). But the record holder, which was shot in 1912, was even longer. It measured an amazing 32 feet 9.5 inches (10 m). Stretched out, it would be the length of a large school bus. After catching their prey, reticulated pythons wrap their extremely long bodies around their victims. Then they squeeze so tightly that the animals can't breathe and soon suffocate to death.

#79 RETICULATED PYTHON:
Longest Snake

#80 RUPPELL'S GRIFFON: Highest-Flying Bird

Ruppell's griffon is a large vulture with a long neck and smallish head. It flies very high over the plains of West Africa. From extremely lofty heights, it uses its exceptionally keen eyesight to find the dead animals, called carrion, on which it feeds. The Ruppell's griffon set the record for highest-flying bird in a tragic way. It was killed by a jet airplane in flight about 7 miles (11 km) above Earth's surface, proving that this griffon could fly at least that high.

The sailfish is generally considered the swiftest swimmer in the sea. Its actual speed, however, is hard to measure. At various times, the streamlined sailfish was clocked at a top speed of 68 miles an hour (109 kph). That is even faster than a cheetah on land! The spectacular fin that stretches nearly the length of its body gives the sailfish its name. Found near the ocean's surface, these fish often use their sails to herd schools of small fish together.

#81 SAILFISH: Fastest Fish

#82 SALTWATER CROCODILE: Largest Reptile

Among today's living reptiles, the saltwater crocodile is the biggest. The record breakers include a 21-foot (6.4-m) saltwater crocodile captured alive in 2011 and several that weighed about 2,350 pounds (1,065 kg) each. Due to their massive size and strength, saltwater crocodiles are able to attack large animals such as water buffalo, wild boars, and kangaroos. They are said to be the animals most likely to attack and eat humans.

Sea horses are exceptionally poor swimmers that move through the water in a straight up-and-down position. Few of them even try to swim against a flowing current. In the shallow tropical and temperate waters where they live, sea horses spend most of their time holding on to sea grass or coral with their tails. In calm waters, these fish swim by fluttering their tiny rear fins. Their estimated speed is only about 50 feet (15 m) an hour!

#83 SEA HORSE: *Slowest Fish*

#84 SEA WASP: Most Poisonous Sea Creature

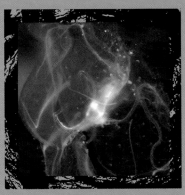

The beautiful, but deadly, sea wasp is the most venomous animal in the sea—or perhaps the entire world! Found only in waters near Australia and parts of Southeast Asia, the sea wasp is sometimes called a box jellyfish. Millions of stinging cells, like tiny darts, cover its long, flowing, stringy tentacles. One wasp contains enough venom to kill 60 people! Just touching a tentacle causes unbearable pain. Many die within minutes of being stung.

The length of a frog's jump is usually the sum total of three jumps in a row. On May 21, 1977, the record for longest jump was set by a sharp-nosed frog of South Africa. It covered an amazing 33 feet 5.5 inches (10 m) in one giant triple jump! That's more than half the distance from home plate to the pitcher's mound on a baseball diamond. Very long, strong rear limbs, and a pointy nose to cut down air resistance, help make this frog a champion jumper.

#85 SHARP-NOSED FROG:
Longest-Jumping Frog

*86 SIBERIAN SALAMANDER: Hardiest Amphibian

The Siberian salamander is one of the only amphibians that live in forests and grasslands inside the frigid Arctic Circle. This amazing animal can survive temperatures as low as -50 degrees F (-45°C)! That's much colder than the temperature in your home freezer. The Siberian salamander can live in such harsh conditions because of a chemical in its cells that is like the antifreeze in a car. It lowers the freezing point of the water in the cells and keeps them from turning to ice.

Giant Siberian tigers live in the vast woodlands of Russia, China, and North Korea. These large, powerful animals can measure up to 10 feet 10 inches (3.3 m) in length and weigh 675 pounds (306.5 kg). However, an all-time record-breaking Siberian tiger that was shot in 1950 weighed a hefty 846.5 pounds (384 kg)! Siberian tigers are known to travel many miles in search of elk, wild boar, and other prey. They lie in wait for victims and then attack with a quick, fatal pounce.

#87 SIBERIAN TIGER:
Biggest Cat

#88 SKUNK: Smelliest Mammal

The skunk is best known for its extremely foul-smelling spray. It is usually a skunk's last defense against predators. When in danger, a skunk first tries to run away, though its short, stubby legs are not built for speed. Next the skunk arches its back, lifts its tail, and stomps its feet to scare away the enemy. If all this fails, the skunk turns around and blasts its foe with the spray, which travels about 10 feet (3 m). Skunk spray doesn't harm anyone, but it sure does stink!

The sooty tern flies for several years without stopping—even sleeping in flight! Its very long journey starts when the young bird flies out of its nest on an island near Florida. From there, it heads east across the Atlantic Ocean to Africa, while feeding on fish and squid that it grabs from the water. At the end of three or more years in the air, the sooty tern is old enough to breed as an adult. It returns to its nesting area where the females lay eggs and the life cycle begins again.

#89 SOOTY TERN: Most Time in the Air

#90 SPERM WHALE: Deepest Diver

Sperm whales live in all the oceans of the world, where they dive as deep as 4,000 feet (1,200 m). At this depth, they can stay down as long as two hours hunting squid—their favorite food. Sperm whales rank first in size among all meat-eating mammals. Some grow as long as 60 feet (18 m) and weigh 60 tons (55,000 kg). Their huge, boxlike heads are about one-third their body length and their gigantic brains are the biggest of any living animal.

The spitting cobra does not bite in defense like most poisonous snakes. It "spits" at its enemies. In fact, it takes the prize for sending its venom the farthest and with the greatest accuracy. The poison spurts out from two small holes near the tips of its fangs. Aimed at the enemy's eyes, it almost always hits the target—even at distances up to 10 feet (3 m)! The poison usually stings and burns the eyes. If not washed out quickly, it can blind the victim.

#91 SPITTING COBRA: Champion Spitter

#92 SPRINGBOK: Best Jumper

Springboks are the champion jumpers of the animal world! Their name comes from the way they shoot straight up into the air, over and over again, without seeming to touch the ground. They often reach heights of about 13 feet (4 m). No one knows why springboks bounce up and down this way. Most think it is to show off their strength and fitness. It is a common sight to see springboks leaping together (called pronking) on the plains of southern Africa.

The stonefish is the most treacherous fish for humans. It usually rests, well hidden, on the ocean bottom in the shallow waters along the coast of Australia. With its brownish color, it looks like a stone, which is where it got its name. When the stonefish is threatened, thirteen needlelike spines straighten along its back. Each spine is attached to a tiny sac of deadly poison, or venom. Anyone unlucky enough to step on the stonefish gets a full dose of extremely deadly poison.

#93 STONEFISH: Deadliest Ocean Fish

94 TERMITES: Greatest Builder Insects

Of all land creatures, termites build the largest structures, called mounds. They build these mounds out of soil, saliva, and their own droppings. The biggest ones are found in northern Australia and Africa, where they can be as high as 20 feet (6 m) and measure 102 feet (31 m) across at the base. The hard, thick walls are perfect for cooling and sealing in moisture. As many as 2 million termites live in tunnels that they dig beneath the mounds.

The three-toed sloth of tropical South America is slow in almost every way. It crawls on tree branches at about 15 feet (4.6 m) a minute and has an on-ground speed of only 6 to 8 feet (1.8 to 2.4 m) a minute. In fact, sloths move so slowly that algae grow on their coats, just as they do on rocks! Three-toed sloths do nearly everything hanging upside down from a tree branch. This includes moving about, eating, sleeping, and even giving birth.

#95 THREE-TOED SLOTH:
Slowest Mammal

#96 TIGER BEETLE: Swiftest Land Insect

No insect runs faster on the ground than the tiger beetle. It's been clocked at 5.5 miles per hour (9 kph)! If the beetle was the size of a human, it would be able to run an amazing 480 miles an hour (772 kph)! The tiger beetle uses its great speed to hunt like a tiger, its ferocious namesake. After finding insect prey, the tiger beetle sets off on a high-speed chase until it runs the bug down. In a flash, the tiger beetle pounces and tears the victim to shreds.

Vampire bats are the only mammals that feed entirely on the blood of other mammals. They need one or two tablespoons of blood every day to survive. The bats are most active on dark, moonless nights. Sleeping cattle and horses in South and Central America are their usual victims. Vampire bats take about 20 to 30 minutes to lap up a day's supply of blood. Victims rarely awaken because the bats' teeth are so sharp that their bite is painless.

#97 VAMPIRE BAT: Most Bloodthirsty Mammal

#98 WANDERING ALBATROSS: Largest Wingspan

The wandering albatross has a record-breaking wingspan of 11 feet 11 inches (3.6 m). That is about the length of a midsize room. This majestic seabird spends much of its time in flight, gliding over ocean waters on winds and updrafts of air. It rarely flaps its wings, yet it covers more than 300 miles (480 km) a day. From time to time, the wandering albatross sets down on the water to feed on squid, fish, or food dumped from ships.

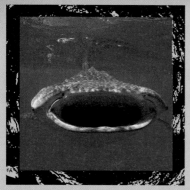

While there have been reports of 59-foot-long (18-m-long) whale sharks, the longest confirmed was 41.5 feet (12.6 m). As you can imagine, these huge animals are very difficult to weigh. But experts estimate that each one is at least 10 tons (9,000 kg). Despite their gigantic size, whale sharks are gentle, harmless creatures. They swim in warm oceans all over the world and mostly eat tiny plants and animals, called plankton, that float in the water.

#99 WHALE SHARK: *Largest Fish*

#100 WILD WATER BUFFALO: Longest Horns

The wild water buffalo of Southeast Asia has the most stupendous horns. They curve out and back from the animal's head in two semicircles. Both male and female buffalo have them. The record for longest horns was set in 1955. A male water buffalo was found with horns that reached 13 feet 11 inches (4.2 m) along the outside curve! The horns on all wild water buffalo get longer as the animals grow older.

Wolverines are as big as medium-sized dogs, but far stronger than any animal of similar size. A full-grown wolverine has razor-sharp teeth and a more powerful bite than a grizzly bear. Wolverines have been known to kill prey as large as moose or reindeer. They often drag dead prey, several times their own weight, for many miles (km). Some even distract big bears by biting them on the back while they are eating—and then steal their food!

#101 WOLVERINE: Strongest for Its Size

INDEX

PHOTO CREDITS

Front Cover: Numbers: top left: SeDmi/Shutterstock, top center and top right: iStockphoto; Animals: top row (left to right): Geoffrey Kuchera/Shutterstock, Mircea Bezergheanu/Shutterstock, Timothy Craig Lubcke/Shutterstock, Cristopher McRae/Shutterstock, Johan Swanepoel/Shutterstock; middle row (left to right): Smileus/Shutterstock, Kitch Bain/Shutterstock, hironai/Shutterstock, Jill Lang/Shutterstock; bottom row (left to right): Sergey Uryadnikov/Shutterstock, Sebastian Duda/Shutterstock, Dirk Ercken/Shutterstock, Roman Sigaev/Shutterstock, Shutterstock; **Back Cover:** Animals: top row (left to right): Karel Gallas/Shutterstock, Gary Bell/SeaPics.com, Jonmilines/Dreamstime; middle row (left to right): covenant/Shutterstock, Lee Torrens/Shutterstock; bottom row (left to right): Stu Porter/Shutterstock, Iv Nikolny/Shutterstock, Stu Porter/Shutterstock; **Interior:** 4t: Pete Oxford/Nature Picture Library; 4b: Morley Read/Nature Picture Library; 5t: iStockphoto; 5b: Martin Maritz/Shutterstock; 6t: Africapics/Dreamstime; 6b: Frank van Egmond/Alamy; 7t: David M. Dennis/Animals Animals; 7b: Vladvitek/Dreamstime; 8t: Christopher Liao/Dreamstime; 8b: Kim Taylor/Nature Picture Library; 9t: OlegDoroshin/Shutterstock; 9b: Hlavkom/Dreamstime; 10t: Rzs/Dreamstime; 10b: Stephen Dalton/Nature Picture Library; 11t: Don Mammoser/Alamy; 11b: Gatito33/Dreamstime; 12t: Songbird839/Dreamstime; 12b: Kane513/Shutterstock; 13t: Joe McDonald/Corbis; 13b: Pwollinga/Dreamstime; 14 (both): photoshot; 15t: blickwinkel/Alamy; 15b: Mgkuijpers/Dreamstime; 16t: Eugenesim/Dreamstime; 16b: Alex Kerstitch/Visuals Unlimited/Corbis; 17t: Denis Scott/Corbis; 17b: Phillip Colla/SeaPics.com; 18t: Mschalke/Dreamstime; 18b: Jeffrey L. Rotman/Corbis; 19t: Steve Knell/Nature Picture Library; 19b: Nstanev/Dreamstime; 20t: Dr. Merlin D. Tuttle/Bat Conservation International/Photo Researchers, Inc.; 20b: Dr. Merlin D. Tuttle/Photo Researchers, Inc.; 21 (both): Hilary Jeffkins/Nature Picture Library; 22t: Starper/Dreamstime; 22b: John Mitchell/Getty Images; 23t: photoshot; 23b: Melonesaj/Dreamstime; 24t: Photowitch/Dreamstime; 24b: Dennis Donohue/Shutterstock; 25t: Tom Brakefield/Corbis; 25b: Markbeckwith/Dreamstime; 26t: Robinrwinkelman/Dreamstime; 26b: DLILLC/Corbis; 27t: Ardea/Lucas, Ken/Animals Animals; 27b: Natural Visions/Alamy; 28t: Dave Allen Photography/Shutterstock; 28b: Kirsanov/Shuttertstock; 29t: David Fleetham/Nature Picture Library; 29b: James Dawson/Dreamstime; 30t: iStockphoto; 30b: A & J Visage/Alamy; 31t: photoshot; 31b: Starper/Dreamstime; 32t: Gsukhanov/Dreamstime; 32b: Corbis RF/Alamy; 33t: Tim Zurowski/All Canada Photos/Corbis; 33b: B2t/Dreamstime; 34t: Ribe/Dreamstime; 34b: D.R. Schrichte/SeaPics.com; 35t: ANT Photo Library/Photo Researchers, Inc.; 35b: Vladsilver/Dreamstime; 36t: Starper/Dreamstime; 36b: Robert Harding; 37: Dr. Harold Rose/Science Source; 38t: Photoshot Holdings Ltd/Alamy; 38b: Solvin Zankl/NPL/Minden Pictures; 39t: WaterFrame/Alamy; 39b: Anthony Pierce/SeaPics.com; 40t: Gorshkov13/Dreamstime; 40b: Mark